leaves an indelible mark on one's work and imagination.

The Beautiful Strangers, which seeks to lead us out of the Me Generation and into a new era of altruism and interdependence, may well be Rod McKuen's most forthright and prophetic book to date.

About the Author

Rod McKuen has traveled throughout the world pursuing more than a dozen occupations—although he is best known as a poet, composer, lecturer and performer. As recipient of the 1978 Carl Sandburg Award, he was acclaimed "the people's poet—because he has made poetry a part of so many people's lives." McKuen's books have sold in excess of 33 million copies and his work is taught and studied in schools, colleges, universities and seminaries the world over.

When not traveling, Rod McKuen spends most of his time in a rambling Spanish house in Southern California or in a New York apartment overlooking the Manhattan skyline. At present he is working on a play.

the
beautiful
strangers

BY ROD McKUEN

BOOKS

PROSE
FINDING MY FATHER
AN OUTSTRETCHED HAND
A BOOK OF DAYS

POETRY
AND AUTUMN CAME
STANYAN STREET & OTHER
  SORROWS
LISTEN TO THE WARM
LONESOME CITIES
IN SOMEONE'S SHADOW
CAUGHT IN THE QUIET
FIELDS OF WONDER
AND TO EACH SEASON
COME TO ME IN SILENCE
MOMENT TO MOMENT
CELEBRATIONS OF THE HEART
BEYOND THE BOARDWALK
THE SEA AROUND ME
COMING CLOSE TO THE EARTH
WE TOUCH THE SKY
THE POWER BRIGHT AND
  SHINING
THE BEAUTIFUL STRANGERS

COLLECTED POEMS
TWELVE YEARS OF CHRISTMAS
A MAN ALONE
WITH LOVE . . .
THE CAROLS OF CHRISTMAS
SEASONS IN THE SUN

ALONE
*THE ROD MC KUEN OMNIBUS
HAND IN HAND
LOVE'S BEEN GOOD TO ME
LOOKING FOR A FRIEND
TOO MANY MIDNIGHTS

MUSIC COLLECTIONS
THE MC KUEN/SINATRA
  SONGBOOK
NEW BALLADS
AT CARNEGIE HALL
MC KUEN/BREL:
  COLLABORATION
28 GREATEST HITS
JEAN AND OTHER NICE THINGS
MC KUEN COUNTRY
THROUGH EUROPEAN WINDOWS
GREATEST HITS, VOL. I
GREATEST HITS, VOL. II

MAJOR FILM SCORES
THE PRIME OF MISS JEAN BRODIE
A BOY NAMED CHARLIE BROWN
JOANNA
THE UNKNOWN WAR
DISNEY'S SCANDALOUS JOHN
THE BORROWERS
LISA BRIGHT AND DARK
EMILY
STEINBECK'S TRAVELS WITH
  CHARLEY

* Available only in Great Britain

CLASSICAL MUSIC

Ballet
AMERICANA, R.F.D.
POINT/COUNTERPOINT
SEVEN ELIZABETHAN DANCES
THE MINOTAUR (MAN TO
  HIMSELF)
VOLGA SONG
FULL CIRCLE
THE PLAINS OF MY COUNTRY
DANCE YOUR ASS OFF
THE MAN WHO TRACKED THE
  STARS

Opera
THE BLACK EAGLE

Concertos
FOR PIANO & ORCHESTRA
FOR CELLO & ORCHESTRA
FOR ORCHESTRA & VOICE
FOR GUITAR & ORCHESTRA
#2 FOR PIANO & ORCHESTRA
FOR FOUR HARPSICHORDS
SEASCAPES FOR PIANO

Symphonies, Symphonic Suites, etc.
SYMPHONY NO. 1
SYMPHONY NO. 2
BALLAD OF DISTANCES
THE CITY
SYMPHONY NO. 3
SYMPHONY NO. 4
4 QUARTETS FOR PIANO &
  STRINGS
4 TRIOS FOR PIANO & STRINGS
ADAGIO FOR HARP & STRINGS
RIGADOON FOR ORCHESTRA

the
beautiful
strangers

ROD McKUEN

CHEVAL BOOKS
SIMON AND SCHUSTER
NEW YORK

PHOTO CREDITS

Author's collection—pages 11, 174.
Simon Metz—pages 20, 46, 60, 92, 97, 131, 159, 164, 170.
Catherine Shaw—pages 4, 57, 106, 120, 134.

DESIGNED BY EVE METZ

MANUFACTURED IN THE UNITED STATES OF AMERICA

10   9   8   7   6   5   4   3   2   1

ISBN: 0-671-43614-7

Further information may be obtained by contacting the Cheval/Stanyan Comp[any]
8440 Santa Monica Boulevard, Los Angeles, California 90069

Some of the material in this book has previously appeared in *Coldspring Jour[nal,]*
Throg, Christian Science Monitor, The Journal of Journeys and *Rod McKuen's F[...]*

FOR
ALL THE BEAUTIFUL STRANGERS

contents

part the first:
designer genes

FOR HELEN BRANN

THEY FIND YOU

They find you in the darkest night
in all the central parks,
at every shopping center mall,
along each stitched-up lane
and bowed, leafytree cotillion,
in the school, pool, fool-around rooms,
and at the smelly deli,
where tired office workers
nightly order carrot salad
and chickens from a spit.
Inside, outside,
they find you.

As each river
never fails to meet its ocean
as water levels into water
and earth goes back to earth again
so too, people of like needs
find and find out about each other.
However long the wait.

Should you travel from yourself,
beginning your ascent/descent
                    toward eternity
before the final door is closed,
the last mile hiked,
like as not they'll find you.

Even those still unaware
that they've been lost
and those too occupied
to see the searcher coming
            and look up
will not be left
somewhere between the dark
            and sunlight.
They too will be uncovered
            and found out.

So it is that life
takes care of us
if we will let it.
Be not afraid, they find you.

Always waiting is a risk.
Whole lifetimes,
even if they last but minutes,
are lost and not regained
while we depend on others
to be the foragers and pioneers.

All of us are prospectors
fossicking for love
                    tunneling through
the terminals of time,
little more than evening vespers.
Perhaps we underestimate our worth
for there are strangers out there
strong and warm and beautiful
                    who look for us.

Do not wait.
Love is not so much
        a double street
as it is a multi-colored maze.

Hide-and-seek is a single game
as finders and the found
are the same sides of a single coin
tossed in the air and spinning.
There are no losers
when everyone is bent on winning.
And if you go out
looking for them
surely *they* will find *you*
sooner than expected.

A FIELD GUIDE TO CRUISING

1.

Smile more often
in the arena or the L-shaped room.
A sense of humor
(especially about one's self)
is rare in this decade
of longing and long faces.

Do not dress up or down
but as you would for an occasion.
With some luck and some premeditation
                              it will be one.

Avoid church socials or the Bake-off.
Those who gather at such gatherings
have paired off long ago.
They are in the middle
              of what they perceive
as the act of living life,
who are we to interrupt them?

Threesomes are as out as ever.
Anything that can be done by three
can be accomplished in a better way by two.
And yet, a second in a singles bar
                              is time wasted,
those there are there
for all the wrong reasons.
Mixed doubles, stringing along
in search of high strung string quartets.
Psychiatrists on leaves of absence.
Stewardesses on one last fling
                              before the Phoenix run.
Businessmen and women out for business.

I suppose for some
leather bars are nice
if you're into costumes
            or bedding down
with fire and ice.

"The best, a moving toward eternity."

Parks are pleasant,
after ten and before four.
My brother picks up sunshine there
                even on the darkest day.
He prefers the daylight.
You can see into a woman's eyes, he says.

About eyes.
If you have not yet learned to grin,
a smiling eye will give
                a quicker answer.
Be not afraid to look directly
                into a stranger's eye.
The worst thing that can happen
is a look away from you.
The best, a moving toward eternity.

2.

If you are under twenty
and call the country home
there's the horseshoe meet, the county fair,
the hayride, and the day side of your life.
You needn't rush or brush past anything
                    without the testament of *try*.
What I mean is—
while the fast lane gets you there
                    the soonest,
the outside lane cannot be ignored
especially if you're not sure where
                    there is.

See the sideshow, then move on
unless you feel you've found
the better breed of freaks
that you went looking for
          the first time out.

Edward says—
my brother speaks again—
that he's been picked up on the street
                by women twice his age,
beautiful women who glide toward him
out of the dreams of dozens of days
                        yardfuls of years
and duos and trios of decades passing.
They come, he says,
not in a gallop of desperation
but slow enough to float along
        on clouds of confidence.

Edward has the street cruise
                down to a science.
I won't tell all his secrets
except to say that he walks slowly
and has a certain walk.

Just past twenty
there's the country bar and grill
in urban or in wildwood settings.
While there are still *coal miner's daughters*
                              to be found,
learn the faces of the local shotgun fathers
before you lead a partner to the call
                              of *do-si-do*.

You streetwise, city men and women,
who long ago left hopscotch games,
don't dally at the disco now
especially while the sun remains your friend.
The end of any/every city block
                    could be for you Lands End.

Passing thirty
don't be fooled by editors and experts
who tell you that you now approach your prime.
Your prime is not your time alone
it is that well-honed, well-heeled hour
you arrive at some destination
                    where the sharer waits.
But, oh, the shine of that decade
that starts the final night of twenty-nine
when we are not yet old enough
for such silliness as cynicism
but too old to run home
everytime the darkness brings
                    a small defeat.
Then ending on the last full eve
                    of thirty-nine,
life starts to rush at you,
a change from all the years
you went on rushing life.

3.

A word to all you younger ladies:
don't be chained by movie stars
and Wella Balsam–girl beliefs.
Hold out your arms
now and again to older men,
we of the tri-colored temples,
softer stomachs
          and wider hands.
All of us have engines that still run,
our mileage down the road
or round the track
has kept us finely tuned
like jaunty Jeeps or ritzy Rolls.
Despite what television tells you
we don't fold up and go to sleep
                              ahead of you.
We wait. As you have waited.

After forty
don't dress up
as though you're twenty-five
and don't fall into feeling
you're lucky to be living.

You might decide to diet
                    once a week.
Join a gym. Stretch.
Swim or run . . . but with eyes open.
Don't be afraid.
This is the magic time
when rhyme falls into reason.
Why feel ill-at-ease, depressed,
unless you get off on delusion—
maybe your illusions need a rest.

But fifty's coming, sixty too.
These are the royal years
when people seek you out
                in your own bedroom.
No need to walk the street
or speak at testimonials.
All over town the young are giving
                testimonials to you.

By now you've long ago
                run out of businesscards.
Start spreading heavenly rumors
                about yourself,
anonymously, of course.
Have flyers printed.
Rent the Goodyear blimp.

To those who feel
they've failed too often
to qualify for Mr. Right,
I hope you've been collecting hats
                along life's runway.
If so, throw another into the ring
let it do your singing for you.

Jezebel, Jazz Baby, or plain Jane,
                        you need not be cunning,
stick out your foot and trip a man
when he comes jogging, running by.
Believe me, we are easily tripped
having waited for the trip so long.

To cruise
is to be considerate.
Unless you call attention
                    to your presence
who will know you're there?

Even a country
has to weave and wave a flag
as proof of its existence.

THE DAY BEFORE THE FORTY-EIGHTH

A table with wooden legs.
She waves her hand and the snowbird flies.
I wave my hand and nothing happens.
I leave off living. I leave off living.
A bang, a clang, a steel-beam belch. A building begins.
I pick up living where I left off.
The moon bleeds. Is no one looking?
The building stumbles, sags, and falls.
Dollars die in my brother's pocket.
A woman runs from the sea.
The rubble is cleared, the building reassembled.
God's erector-set is working.
Her face is a rumor, gossip only.
She waves her hand and nothing happens.
I wave my hand and the snowbird flies.

Gulls in the awnings pick at the eaves.
Earthworms suck at the cobblestones.
She slips into coma and cobweb tangle.
Her spirit slides through the door.
It has rained too long.
The season is changing from winter into winter.
The building has grown higher
while my head was turned away.
She flails at me. I do not argue.
Work is up to my waist and piling.
The moon is bandaged. Condition stable.
She wakes and waves. I do not acknowledge.
My brother is having his hardest day.
I'm unable even to make a list
of what I should or should not be doing.

I read the *Times*, drink water, squander money.
I've convinced my friends I *am* living again.
The mirror rattles, a truck is passing.
A horse with blinders paws at the door.
The ailing moon still nurses her wound.
She opens her mouth to speak and screams.
I help my brother past his forty-fifth.
He hoards his change in an eagle bottle.
The building adds another story every other day.
I realize that to help my brother
I should have learned to help myself.
The horse is pacified, feedbag on.
Gulls have flown, earthworms tunneled.
The elevator opens, I glimpse God.
Time is an elephant stripping branches.

The building is finished, topped by a flag.
I take up a language and come away mumbling.
My brother has finally gone to the gym.
I circle the circles I've already made
retracing my steps within the same hour.
The moon is cured of mysterious ailments.
My arm grows tired from waving my hand.
Baggage comes out and I start to unpack.
Yesterday's dreams don't work anymore.
She smiles. She knows. She always did.
I face the mirror and inhale failure,
I exhale and the mirror cracks.
I chip the corners of crystal blocks.
Whatever I touch is meant to be flawed
And so I make no plans for tomorrow.

The scaffolding's gone from the ongoing building.
My brother unlocks the door and comes home.
April is leaving with all it embraced.
The girl passes by, her hands in her pockets.
I drop a language and pick up a stone.
Stones are not given to misrepresentation.
The moon is as dull as coins without silver.
I stare at the telephone alive with silence.
I am wasting time, keeping track of time wasted.
A girl is laughing. The room gets smaller.
I count out a dollar in nickels and dimes.
Nobody pays attention to warnings.
A cluttered table with wooden legs.
An obstacle between me and tomorrow.
People move in, the new building grows old.

DESIGNER GENES

With laissez-faire each derriere
with nom or nom de plume
is held in place with little space
to wiggle or sha-boom.

Though upper class, with hips en masse
may swoon or merely moan
the denim set does not abet
though Sassoon sues Sasson.

Francophile in cut and style
and lusty ambiance
hello, goodbye, Bon Jour for sure
is just a pair of pants.

For those unyoung
who would be built
Glorioski! Vanderbilt.

For thighs the size
of shepherd's crook
three guys devised
the Jordache look.

Some new fanglers
with longer danglers
prefer, I'm sure
the lure of Wranglers.

Jesse Jeans, a better bet
for punning than for running
jumping, standing still, or passing twenty.
In singles bars spot would-be stars
in Sergio Valente.

If it's the gods
who choose the bods
to illustrate each line
the lord must be decidedly
a clone of Calvin Klein.

Double-stitched and TV pitched
in boardroom or bunkhouse
hip, hip hooray, a toast we say
to Levi and to Strauss.

Who knows what crazed couturiers
await to trip their trap
or slip the invite through the gate
Come! Fall into the Gap.

Sad but true, blood may run blue
in veins of kings and queens
but outwardly, true royalty
reigns in designer genes.

With so much green
from selling jean
the market's far from thinning
pegged or flair, both get their share
the end is the beginning.

PENSIONER

Deprived of cats and children
and now her eyes begin to go.
Fetch my glasses from the dresser
                              or wherever
she calls out to me.
I do so out of habit
cleaning each lens with my shirttail
as I bring the dimestore plastic
to her steady hands.

She is now past needlepoint
and any need for old friends dropping by.
They interrupt my television, she says to me.
Double lock the door before you go.

I do. And think as I go down the walk,
I will not watch this woman,
        though no kin of mine,
be folded over like a day bed
and trucked away to Leisureland
robbed of her own magazine-stacked rooms.

I've heard the mutterings of her brother
            and an aging aunt
(who seem to be not altogether
                    held together
more like marionettes
with much string missing).
They make plans to steal her
on some unwitting night
and take her on a

                cross-trip.
            ghetto-town

It would be a comfort
if I thought they were well-meaning.
                    They are not.
I've noticed sometimes when I visit
and find the aunt or brother there
that even when they speak to her
their eyes are on a dusty trunk
that looks as though its hinges
have remained unused for decades.
I imagine them imagining the divvy
                    of the spoils inside.

The joke's on them.
Sensing their manuever long ago
she's weaseled quarters, dimes and dollars
out of these irrelevant relatives' pockets.
for sustenance and subscriptions
              to years of *TV Guide*
by letting them suspect the trunk holds treasure.

Indeed if there was treasure
                    to be had
the government ran off with it
a dozen years ago.
More magazines and pictures
of an only husband hide behind the lock,
not stocks or bonds or bricks of gold.
And stuffed between her mattress and the world
is a pillow of some age
                    and little substance
to keep the cold out on the chilly night.

We have a pact, we two.
I bring a lock each time I visit
and flush the old key down the toilet.
I hide the new one
in one more not-too-secret niche
and snap the new lock on the old trunk shut,
pocketing last week's padlock.

Six keys have turned up missing
                    in as many years—
through half-closed eyelids, feigning sleep
she watched as each was seen and snatched
by he or she who made the latest
                              obligatory visit.

On Thursdays we take schnapps together
and giggle at the prospect
of the grand opening of her hope chest
                              once she's gone—
the brother hovering, the aunt all fingers.

This imagined scene
had been replayed between us
in a dozen variations until last week.

On Tuesday last her brother died,
more from meanness than old age.
The aunt was willed his share of keys.
The ecstasy of such good fortune
proved too much for her, alas.
She too expired when told the news.

Just as well.
I had run out of padlocks
or money to buy them.
Next visit we will have to think up
                         brand new game.

"The winter has widened ..."

WOMEN IN WINTER
(A Second Look)

The winter has widened
                    and it won't be easy.
Nearly everywhere the city's closing up.
Old women come down to the park
their hands withered, gnarled, broken—
scarves and handkerchiefs wrapped round
                                    and round them
offer no protection.
But they have to rise
from their empty lifeless beds
and shuffle through the streets to prove
the hours left to them
are hours of importance.
Hours they can hold between
their aching winter fingers.

Here in the park
the pigeons and the snowbirds wait
knowing their arrival
is constant as the clock
and those slow moving women
bring the most delicious crumbs
and bits of bread
from bottom bags.

Through the years
these ladies of the lolly
and the crumpled crumb
have mastered each bird's language.

Even in the ice-bound streets
when no one else dares venture out
they thread their way like
                    mystic maidens
through their ranks of cooing children
                    till each is fed and flies.

Disappearing with a crust, a crumb
                    a croissant halved or quartered,
these snowbirds fly on angel wings
dipping to salute the earthbound goddesses
who offered sustenance and salvation.

ADVICE TO THE RIVER

River
don't flow
past yourself.
Around the bend
waits more of you
    and nothing more.

NICKI'S FIRST SNOW

Nicki had been sitting in the window
attracted by a trapped-in moth
now pawing at the dirty glass,
           now batting in midair
absorbed in feline wonder
by a nightbug ill-equipped for daylight.

I look away a moment.
Looking back, I see that Nicki
           has become quite still.
Rapt and silent,
he watches a steady wall of snow
descend like silver serpentine
           or cellophane confetti.

Suddenly he jumps down
with his usual grunt,
as though it were an effort—
proving it isn't
            by landing like a feather.
Then turning with a whispered half-meow,
he signals me to open wide the door.
I do and out he bounds,
then bounds back backward
                    just as quickly,
leaving four small pawprints
on the otherwise untrafficked terrace.

Now gingerly as kings go forth to battle
                    at the rear of armies
brave Nicki tests the terrace yet again—
one paw extended and put down
then just as quickly pulled back in,
he turns to look at me again
and frowns because I'm smiling.

I reach across the table
                    for a rubber ball,
an old one I've discovered lately
in one of his not-quite-so-secret
                              hiding places.
I toss it through the air.
His eyes arch with it as it flies.

The ball lands on the terrace
skidding through the snow
                    then stopping
with the kind of force
a knowing child uses to rein in his sled
at the end of some long,
much too slow toboggan ride.

Go get it Nicki, I call confidentially
as though I've deigned to share a secret.

The cat will not be taken in.
He only looks at me as if to say
how dare you toss a treasure
            not even yours to toss
into some alien land.
And then as if to punctuate
            his statement,
he trots off to the bedroom
and the double bed he shares with me.
Another grunt and he's curled up
and on his way to a proper sleep.

So much for little wonders
like the birth of slow October snow.

A cat's interest
in something disagreeable to him
comes and goes as quickly
as the blinking eye of eagles.

Anyway, with winter only starting
Nicki's got enough time up ahead
to build a proper snowman,
and one more excuse
each time the ground goes white
          to have another nap.

TURN, TURN, TURN

Red and gold brocade
has finally penetrated every tree—
            maple and not maple—
as this too long autumn goes on
                            hanging on.

A few more days
and squirrels will begin dislodging
                    stored-up nuts
thinking fall has merged with spring
passing over winter in its haste,
already new grass grabs at riverbanks
and sneaks, pale yellow,
from beneath dead stones.

While autumn lingers undecided
as to when to finally go
the breath of winter
rounds the corners.

First gold
and then the red brocade
begins to form a carpet
                for the snow.

part the second:
cloud valley

FOR CAROLINE LAWS

CLOUD VALLEY

for Gabriel

Clouds like crumpled handkerchiefs
expand, retract, and then again expand
                            within a crowded sky.
Trees are younger here, roads longer.
Even telephone lines seem more finely tuned
so that their hum is not unlike
bellbirds at the downfield gate.

The deer run free.
They trot in herds,
                all shapes and sizes
lingering and malingering
at the edge of rain forests,
where Spanish moss rides up
                            the tree trunks
and leaps from limb to limb.

"Even telephone lines seem more finely tuned . . ."

At night and every morning
there are rainbows
that erase themselves
even as you run to fetch a camera.
Birds of every color
hang in the air at feeders
waiting in turn for breakfast,
or slip into the forest
to fill their feathered bellies
with a dozen unsuspecting bugs.
I sleep well here
and Gabriel has come down
                    for the weekend.

Caroline and John seem happy—
she of the slow melodious voice
and languid afternoon naps,
he astride his tractor turning earth,
fixing fences with the aid of Link
or feeding endless sugar cubes to Cassanova.

We meet at mealtime
to laugh at nothing
or offer never-ending toasts
                to one another
with South Australian wine.

This turquoise world
feels more like South America
                than New South Wales.
It is altogether too civilized to be civilized.

Gabriel is always smiling
a sly half-European smile.
I think she longs to go back home
                to Florence
and her new Italian lover.
I long for her to stay.
Link, Cloud Valley's clever clown,
addresses all his jokes to her.

This is like some idyll for me
                            being idle
and trying hard to pressure John
to do more writing.

At night, we all play Willie Nelson records,
and make the overseas operators crazy
trying to track down Roger Miller.

Last night and far into the morning
I played for them
the newest version of *Black Eagle*,
filling in the story
in between the tracks.
All day today, John whistled *Flying Free*,
while Casanova neighed softly in the pasture.

How did I
easily the most practicing patriot of my country,
allow Australia so much room inside me?
The tour's been finished for a month
but I go on making up excuses to stay on.

If time was not a trumpet
always sounding out assembly
                    and formation
I'd let the work go whistling
and send out obligations with the garbage,
then sink down into pillows
and find that dozen years of sleep
I've somehow lost,
or go to work for John building,
tearing down, then putting fences
                        up again—
marooned in the sweet monotony
                    of physical motion.

I am marking time
or wasting time
or trapped by time
                or something.
Time and me are Siamese twins—
                        inseparable.

I think it's time
that I began to live
and Cloud Valley, this new
                beautiful stranger,
has things to teach me
if I'll listen.

Just now, the only sound I hear
is the pealing of Australian bellbirds.
Someone's at the downfield gate.

POR FAVOR

Wait for me!
My legs are not as long as yours
and I must run to stay in place.

Speak slower, softer!
My ears are older and your accent thick,
it cuts me off from what you say.

Turn to me.
I have seen so many backs in this lifetime.
Yours, however beautiful
is but another back.

Pray for me.
My sins are many
and at your bidding
may go unpunished
or at least be tempered
in the master's eye.

LOVING ELIZABETH

Having loved you all these years
at distance and close quarters
from the time when you were purple-eyed
and velvet on an English countryside,
through triumphant trips in Tennesseeland,
as the snow fell in Gstaad, as a rainbow arched in Rome,
through husband and husbands and gossip and gloss,
through childhood and girlhood and womanly calm
past Dorchester doorways and limousines waiting
at the curb of California bungalows . . .

In our rooms in Botswana, separate—apart,
I grew and grow up loving you.

Through sickness and sorrow and sandpiper days
and nights when the fire of fear blazed on,
through years without seeing you,
the years when I watched you day after day
playing and posturing
and pouring for others the elixir of love
over my shoulder and out of my reach,
I have loved and love you with unswerving pride.
What I saw with my eyes, what I knew was inside
won all the arguments hearts have with minds,
did the deciding, overriding the lies
that logic holds up as unquestionable truth.

In our rooms in London, separate—apart
I grew and grow up loving you.

TOM AND ANDREW ENTER THE EIGHTIES

1.

She does not merely dance
nor does she float or glide,
                lead or follow.
Being with her on the floor
as the room revolves
requires no talent of her partner.
She evolves, then turns against the tide
of tired and sweating dancers
missing beats and bumping clumsily
as they become entrapped
by one small R.S.V.P. flash
                from her alarming eyes.

Moving with her
I feel like a worker ant
who having carried sustenance
through all the interlocking chambers
of a seven-story anthill
finally comes upon the inner room
                    belonging to the queen.

And now with nothing left to do
I carry out a planned vacation
on the round rim of her smile,
a smile in all ways perfect and complete.

Her energy is catching
        it transmits itself
                in a line direct to me.

We are spinning like a single top
and though held tight
              within her reference
I stay alive and wide awake
even as the dance becomes more automatic
and I sense her scope begin to widen
far beyond my eyes and arms and self.
Those eyes that dart around the room
like flecks of light that bounce
                  from mirrored disco balls
now single out two other bodies bound by motion
for special circumstance and dispensation.

2.

The slighter of the two,
though both are giants,
must be the son of Gulliver—
                    he is introduced as Tom.
Then Gulliver himself appears
huge and dark, a solitary muscle
like the trunk of some
well-cared-for, perfectly pollinated tree.

I watch as they dance
                circles 'round me
till caught as only giants can be
by beauty—sudden, quick, and undemanding
she joins the two
to make a trinity.

Gone, then back again, then gone
                         and back,
a beat is never missed.
Tom passes by and pointing out his friend,
speaks his name as if commanding: *Andrew!*

Aye, and Andrew is imposing,
and now the music swells
as though each piper
down a dozen Scottish fields
had heard his name
and taking up a worn-out tune
                         had made it new again.

Andrew's coming!
Do you not ken his tune
and see his banners
                down the distance?

Every second circle
they pass a vial between them
and as though each smells
                a newly opened rose
their smiles widen
and their heads fly back
and every step grows lighter
as this agile Ariadne leads her minotaurs,
Tom and Andrew, into the middle Eighties.
I follow, but by eyesight only,
the happy voyeur just outside the dance.

With exhaustion
as the only warning,
holding one another up
Goliath, leaning on Goliath,
stumble down the metal stairs
and wrapping heavy coats about them
disappear (by turning for a moment sideways)
through the February winter door.

We linger. Moments only.
Then in the street, I hail a taxi.
The woman turns to wave goodbye and goes.
I nod, but do not raise my arm.

3.

I have beaten water marks
along the beaches of Brazil,
gone seven hundred feet below the earth
to mine the gold of New South Wales,
galloped on a Russian stallion
through forbidden forests
and seen my name blink back at me
a thousand times in places where
none were there who knew my name,
but only once
has time's own mistress
let me tag along with giants
and be content to merely watch
                    and disbelieve,
to wonder and at once be sure.

How do you chronicle
events that have not been
a part of what you term as life
                              before?

There is no time
for going back to school
so I continue moving forward
                    straight ahead,
even on a winter morning
when all else sleeps
except the ghosts of giants
tumbling round and round inside my head.

SOME VOICE

Some inaudible voice
instructs the month of April
and so we have pink blossoms
                    everywhere.

Some secret mouth
that only grass can hear
whispers through the trees in June
and suddenly the grass is tall
                        as reeds.

Some autumn finger
a hand connected to an arm
invisible to everyone
                except the sun
moves slow and steady over all the land
commanding everything that grows
                        to die.

So that when the month of April
                comes around again,
some voice inaudible to men
will order trees to blossom,
grass to be reborn,
for man's pleasure and his own.

Some voice that none of us
                are meant to hear
speaks clearly and with sure command
to everything but man.
And so we are assured of one more
                God-made perfect year.

SHOW ME THE WAY TO THE NEXT WHISKEY BAR

I run because there are demons inside me.
I run because there are demons inside you.
I run because there are demons inside everyone.
I run because I run.
I run because.
I run.

AIRPORT CONVERSATION

They were quiet, shy
turning inward on themselves.
It was not that they spoke softly
                in such a noisy place,
they did not speak at all
yet still remained balanced,
teetering on the edge
of some word within a sentence
surrounded by the barbed wire
                of a paragraph.

She, hands folded in her lap.
He, arm raised and then put down
almost in cadence—
                again and then again
waving flies away
in this suspended place
that airlines term a waiting room.

It fell to me
to cut the wire
and set the words to trickle first
and then go rushing
like a torrent of melting snow
                down a too steep hill
swelling the banks of a gully
not quite wide enough.

Squeezed in next to them
I finally knew that silence
would arise and run from us
if I did not puncture it
or tear a corner off.

I smiled.
She asked the proper way to say
a word I could not understand.
I hesitated.

Not important.
You sit with us, please. I did.
We had a drink together, not tea.
Syllables and gestures crawled between us.
An hour passed. Another and more quickly.

Do you have the time, please?

English not good, very.

A watch was shown to me
the sleeve that covered it
remained pulled back
until I nodded in pretense
of making mental notes
at what the clock ticked off.
In truth I marked
        another kind of time.
What now? A smile? A nod?
              I nodded.

My English better, the woman spoke.
Ah, a conversation would begin.

Did I live in Los Angeles?
Would they like Los Angeles?
I did. I thought they would.

The words did not come in a torrent.
No wild river
            overflowed its bounds
but broken sentences
and parts of paragraphs
became a ping-pong narrative
that eased a long
            and getting longer afternoon.

I fight in war before
            Corregidor.
I have medals.
Kill no G.I., he assured me
then repeated, *Kill no G.I.*

I wasn't old enough to go,
but I've seen many pictures:
silence again.

In this wordless time
the woman seemed to become older,
more frail, a little sad.

We go Los Angeles
Bring home only son.
Back to father's house.

He will be glad to see you.
I had stopped speaking
                  in contractions.
They both looked down
and did not raise their eyes again.
I repeated my last sentence.

We do not blame Los Angeles.
Los Angeles fine place, Genko say so.

Genko, good boy.

I'll enjoy meeting him.

Sometimes when quiet
                    interrupts a speech
it does so loud as thunder
rumbling off an echo of an echo
sounding almost engineered.

We are first we know
to lose a boy in Los Angeles
                    In America.
She widened her statement.
I did not reply.
My eyes had settled on a group
                    of missing tiles
that unbalanced a mosaic
otherwise completely perfect
in the corner of the ceiling.

Set in place
with skill and symmetry
they formed a waterfall
that splashed down the wall
to hide behind
a high mosaic hill.
Another tile was missing
                    lower down.
It must have gone unnoticed
by the airport maintenance women
who even now emptied and polished
                    ashtrays
and swept up debris
carefully circumventing the legs
of waiting travelers—
having tea or re-reading magazines
they'd read less carefully an hour before.

The plane was called.
And now the trip would start.

Getting up to go, she speaks.
We know America shoots her children
                              in the street,
America did not have permission
                    to shoot mine.

You come Japan again
            You nice man.

I turned to look across my shoulder.
The water at the bottom of the falls
splashed too far away
for me to count the missing tiles

DESIGNER GENES, REDUX

Not by pre-arrangement did they come,
nor was my birth itself well-planned.
My father, a salesman of sorts,
traveled through Oakland in the 30's,
dallied in a dancehall there
and met my mother for a dime.

Had they not coupled in the dance
and then recoupled in a room somewhere
I might have had less noble blood
than that of dreaming vagabond
                    and ballroom ballerina.

But God is wise beyond all years
and decades he sent driving
                    through the rain
and so I have my father's ears
and on good days my mother's brain.

The body I've been stretched
                   and stitched into
seems flexible enough
         and not in need of patching.
My head, while arguably knowledgeable,
stands firm on steady shoulders.
I've got legs that carry me along
                   with strength and sureness.

Though I'm aware of my designer genes
I have not sewn a label on my chest.
It is enough for me to know
that I was made from equal parts
of love and need and sharing.
It has eclipsed the need
of ever wearing labels.

A TREE

Such frustration comes
                from not knowing
how to take a brush in hand
                  and paint.

To color in the sky
the way an inner eye perceives it
especially in spring,
to translate six or seven blues
                with flecks of green
into the ocean at day's edge,
                      day's end.
To paint and by so doing
                make thinge *be*.

"I wish that I could be
a limb, a root, a bud
of that great giant pine."

Outside my bedroom window
there's a tree
a pine whose brawny branches
have for years
spread speckled shadows
        all across the yard,
a tree whose veins must be
so deep inside the earth
that nourishment for other trees
within its scope is scooped up
by the old pine's taproot
and held for ransom.

A kind of famine there must be
for saplings and the rose
wherever that tree goes tunneling
for sustenance and refuge.

I wish that I could be
a limb, a root, a bud
of that great giant pine.
I wish that I could paint it
truly with a sentence
or a palette of a dozen greens,
for it is more a part of me
than nearly anyone or anything
I've so far encountered.

To share it would be sharing love,
the kind it gives within its shadow
to all who see it.
To share it would be
tantamount to sharing
truths too private to expose
                        till now
with all of those in need
of honesty within the hour.

part the third:
brighton and beyond

FOR WADE ALEXANDER

JOGGER

He's reaching toward fifty
not hitting it head-on, mind you
as he should and knows he should
but reaching out with tentacle-like fingers
toward the middle hundred figure.

Shaking as the year, the month
the day comes closer
insisting that he's unaffected
but looking twice in every passing mirror,
patting several chins and drawing in
                            an extra stomach.

Last week at the beach
he walked by with some children
well, not really children,
but three young girls, each not yet twenty.
Keeps me young, he said, *keeps me young.*

Tentatively his tentacles reach out
toward the day next week
when he pulls back stubs.

I remember one girl saying
        buy me a popsicle.
He would not have recognized
reality on a stick
        and melting.

LOOK FOR THE UNION LABEL

A good quality of worsteds
will endure hard service.
Closely woven fabrics
keep out cold air.
Quality cotton is best grown
on islands off the coasts
              of Georgia.
Satin weave is derived
from the twill weave.
Artificial silks dissolve
or become weakened
        when boiled.
Clothes should both amplify
      and camouflage.

Shoes ought to be inspected
at the end of each day's wear.
Sports clothes are suitable
to wear to the races.
A delicate yet serviceable
bulletproof vest is sometimes worn
                    to the race riots.
Green brings a pinker color
                    to the skin
and reddens already red hair.
The color is also suitable
for combat fatigues
and paratrooper overalls.
And remember, the color orchid
can be safely worn
when lavender is out of the question.

ROLL OF THE DICE

Will it be remembered
      and by who,
that once upon the blackest
      of Castilian nights
we threw stars,
like diamond dice, along the sand?

And once when it grew quiet
you asked, "Is this love?"
Then before I answered
you had framed and put to me
yet another question.

BRIGHTON ONE:
SLEEP AFTER THE LANES, 1971

Saturday night
ducking, dodging
through the Brighton lanes,
pursuing and pursued,

When nothing comes
of conquest of conquistador
the quietude of that same
upstairs room
is like an iron mantle
clamping down and making
every organ useless,

And still sleep doesn't come.

It's then you know
that speech is nothing.
                    Not because
there is no one to speak to
but because yet one more time
you were not chosen
by the chosen
and you did not choose
                    to speak
even though the chosen
might have waited
thinking your words
should come first.

"...those same
blind barricades
that we're erecting"

Why do we study,
why do we become
            learned men?
Why do we cheat
                and force
and push our way
through what we think
are barricades,
when all the while
it is those same
blind barricades
that we're erecting?

When it comes to need
intellect could not be
            more useless
and there's not knowledge
near enough or deep enough
to satisfy or substitute.

With imagination so well worn
that a single sigh is every bit
as powerful as sublimation.
Need can drive you
down the darkest alley
and leave you there,
beached and bloody,
still waiting for
a new encounter.

Need,
and need not gratified
has helped me understand
why the suicide can do it
and how the alcoholic can
transcend and thereby end
                    his limit.

Monday morning,
out of sleep,
too little sleep
that came too late.
The car is waiting.
On to Bournemouth.

Another night of faces
not seen completely
        and not seen again.
There are eyes and forms
that stand out even in the dark.
They become then individuals
                    not audience.
They never know
and I can't tell them.

What if I put the question
to some of those who linger
when the show shuts down
and the answer came back, *no?*

One more bed
in one more room
now sleep hurries in,
even though the senses
still stay poised
for the small
or great adventure.
Tomorrow there's the London train,
a month to go
and then Los Angeles again.

BRIGHTON TWO:
A NEWLY PAINTED BENCH, 1980

Standing, waiting, smiling in the line.
You were patient—while impatiently
                            I moved toward you.
A touch as slight as some single
                            spider's,
a name scrawled in a book
and you were disappearing,
                  fast as the steamy Brighton night
through the crowd, out the door, away
leaving me to go on scrawling.

We knew. My God, we knew
without the running radar eye
whose signal never stopped
even when your back was turned
                  and you no longer looked at me.

Knowing isn't always good enough.
One of us should have been braver.

I cannot say how long it took
for that over-peopled crowd
          to one by one go home.
When I emerged into the new May moonlight
the sidewalk still held faces asking questions,
and bodies with their arms outstretched
for handshakes and hand-holding.

You were there again
sitting silently against the wall
                  upon a painted bench.
I could only smile
perhaps a half-smile, for in it
                      there was deep regret.

How often I've said *no* by saying nothing.
Life is passing with a hundred alternate endings
                              I will never know
because I only travel work to work—
not by choice or even need.
Although I preach the need for one to one
I seldom set in practice my own ethic.
Perhaps on some occasions I write down
                    these little tragedies
so that I'll commit to memory
times and places, fancied forms and faces
not for the reader's sake, but mine.

The heart says *help me*
but it does not say how.
The mind knows all the ways
but will not shift from idle
                    into thinking.

Not knowing, I'm observed, applauded
                          at a distance,
even as I am reaching out.
These arms are never long enough
to reach the sighted but unseen.

I go on traveling like a bullet
on luxury liners and late model limousines.
A cadre still commands my every move,
town to town, performance to performance—
the chance of stepping from the stage
into a pair of waiting, wanting arms
grows more remote the more I grow.

I looked at you. I looked at you,
and if I failed to stride
to where you waited smiling
                on that newly painted bench,
know that I'll regret my indecision
                          all my life.

You were a siren calling me
to some new shining sea,
and I was too wound-up to listen.

And so on Friday night,
May sixteenth, nineteen eighty,
I left Brighton once again
and left behind a form, a face
that I had come a thousand
                    and a thousand
and three thousand miles to find.

As I was driven through the night to London
I sunk down in the backseat of the car
as easily as the dead slip into
newly hollowed graves.

WHY LOVE

It is not just
for our own good pleasure
that we come to love each other,
discovering the differences
divining the sameness
that finally tell us
what we truly are:
selfish in our needs
yet willing to give everything
so that we might please our God
                        not just each other.

For the desperate
God is not the father
but the waiting arms of love.

Love,
as simple as we see it
            on the outside
as complicated as it soon becomes
at closer quarters.

I believe no animal or man,
nothing that depends on contact
within the universe we know
beds down with another of its kind
            in the absence of love.

Some thing
not always something
has to swell the heart
to make things work.

Who among us has come away from love
with nothing but a self reward?
What is left behind,
what sticks and stays
                as we move on
is the part of us that's best.
If we ever wish to see
the best side of ourselves
the side unselfish, unafraid
then we must learn to love.

"...images I've placed
beneath my eyelids
for total recall"

FORCE OF HABIT

I fall in love with pictures
                drawings too.
Christina in that field,
the pantyhose commercial
sandwiched in between
                The World at War
and *War of the Worlds.*

Illustrations illustrate for me
what it is and who it is
                I'm missing.
Women in the act
of putting on and taking off
                transparent clothing.
Men at work
who should be resting.
Loafers I expect to see
move from one page to another
                to shoulder shovels.

Oh, I do dream
and I do love
images I've placed
beneath my eyelids
for total recall or enhanced
                    bring-back
                        as needed.

There is a certain safety
in the packaged bride
or illustrated lover.
Their availability is dependent
only on a given need
at a given time.
They never turn up unexpectedly
and never fail to arrive
precisely when requested.

As such
the would-be groom
        of picture postcards
should be warned
to memorize the sketch and still-life
                        so completely
as to secure for always
the sureness of complete projection
when reality is absent
                or forgets us.

BAJA

Scarlet is the space
that flushes out
the folded cloud lines
in the western sky
between the silent surface
        of the sea.

In only moments
the space will narrow,
grow quite red,
then quiet pink—and go.
And still the old man
does not come
        to lead the cattle home.

Whatever mystery has made him late,
the animals are restless now.
Should I start down the road,
        they'd follow—
Gladly I would lead them home
but by which road?

That seems to be the center,
the heart and edge
        of every quandary.
Which road? When to take it?
How to know for sure.

I have found—
when doubting most—
that up ahead is always up ahead
and however many turns
         the right or left road makes
it always leads to right or left.

I do not imagine
what I've said or say
will offer much encouragement
to the would-be traveler
but the information, once distilled,
              should say
the only way to get there is to go.

PASSING THROUGH

We pass the signs
          the seasons
and the signposts now
at such a speed
that pausing to reflect
on what direction means
grows harder year by year
and yet your God and mine
daily holds his breath
expecting us to listen
and to care about each other.

Across the fields
beyond the highways
and each ocean,
I reach out to you
hoping I'll be welcomed
by another outstretched hand.

For each day
in the year just starting
and all those days in years ahead
I wish you love and reason
          in your life
and most of all
the feeling and reality
of our friendship.

A FIELD GUIDE TO CRUISING, CONT'D.

I forgot about binoculars.
If you home it in a high rise
                    they're a must.
Make sure that they are strong enough
to penetrate the tinted window,
unless it's only naked bodies
on a penthouse sunroof
that you wish to see.

Oh boy, Wade told me
*you should see who came
                    over the fence
and filled up the bird-feeder yesterday.*
And Wade only lives on the first floor.

Binocular cruising is a little difficult.
You search the other high rises
till you find another
looking through a spy-glass
                          straight to you.
Wave slightly. Then feign disinterest.
Even look away a moment
as though you hadn't planned
to be caught in the act.
Look back. Certain actions
(this is a family book and we
needn't go into graphics),
will tell you if there's mutual interest.

Then one of you will hold a card up
with a telephone number printed clearly
in wide felt-tip letters.

If you're the caller
talk in generalities at first.
If you're the callee,
lower your voice an octave—if male.
Females ought to speak in whispers.

If you hear only heavy breathing, hang up.
Or leave the receiver off the hook
and take a shower. Cold.

If you do make contact
it's o.k. to kiss on the first date.

In cruising,
one does not emulate the speckled grouse,
taking one step forward, two steps back.
Go straight ahead. Be assertive.
Particularly if you are an introvert.
If you are an extrovert, cool it
till at least three months
              into the relationship.

Do not accept sweets
              from strangers
no matter how desperate you are.
Supermarkets
have been known to yield
the hunter proper harvest.

Peace rallies used to be
              great for cruising
then the war ended.

part the fourth:
water over stones

FOR YOKO ONO

WATER OVER STONES

I know that death is not so proud
that it will pass my door
leaving me to sort out for myself
departure date and schedules
                    for the train to Styx
or just which chariot will knock me down
within the narrow alley or the busy street
then carry me to heaven by the shortest route.
So I am ready.

I have dwelt upon the death of friends
                              in private
missing public funerals and memorials
(the chance to beat my breast before the crowd
            and shout aloud, *Ah, woe, Ah, me!*)
Ah men, Ah women, Amen is what I said
                              but privately
when friends betrayed me with their deaths.

I will go down death's road alone
and hope to leave behind but one memorial—
a lifeless body that did not acquaint itself
                    with compromise.

"Every day we hold on to life
as much as the living can."

ROUNDABOUT

Every day
we live life to the fullest
we die a little
          but who complains?
Not the man who props his pocket open
to catch an extra share
of unexpected rain.
Not the woman, love exhausted,
told by her lover
that she has never been more beautiful
than those few minutes
lying there half smiling
like the softest breeze
that rattles gently
at the tops of all the tallest trees.
Not the child who after school
was knocked half-winded to the ground
by a fly ball in a favorite game.

Every day we hold on to life
as much as the living can.

Every day we buy a ticket
to somewhere, anywhere.
We travel out of one life
                    into another.
We're always on our way to death.
The hope should be
that we will do what dying must be done
                    on our own ground;
not taking up another's space,
disrupting or disturbing
                    those who love us.

JOHN LENNON, 1940–1980

This man
came *across the universe*
               when needed
crying 'nothing's gonna change
                 my world'
and was taken from it
long before the job
that he invented for himself
                was finished.

The silt that settles in and saddens
erases endings and enrages starts
is not that maniacs continue
to still genius,
it is the knowledge knocked into us
                  yet again
that peace is not with the people
and love cannot, will not be legislated,
It does not spread among us
with the urgency of pestilence or plague.

Lunacy is the new epidemic.
Will there be statistics soon
that tell us madness now strikes
                              one in four?

The widow and the child
the nation and the citizen
                    cannot mourn
and by so doing be relieved.

With presidents and popes
                  and poet minstrels
                        in the crossfire,
who walks in safety?
Not the Georgia child,
not the city subway rider,
not some divided country
believing that it fights a holy war
by sacrificing its people
                    to famine and fast.

It is not enough to hope
                    that ashes
taken by the wind so quickly
will come to earth as seeds,
and new John Lennons will begin to sprout
by the thousands and the thousands.
We must continue to BELIEVE
that many are the men of peace
who from time to time will set out
                    to walk among us.

Even now
as we await, anticipate
the arrival of the newest architect
                    of sensibility
we are late in joining hands
to form a circle of protection for him.

But I have noticed, only recently
that the widows of slain giants
take on a certain afterglow,
or was this the shine
that illuminated those great men
                              before the slayings
seen only now
because the greatness we observed
                              has been removed.
Perhaps it is a partnership,
one we never understood.
                              If so
the half that stayed behind
shines brighter than most constellations,
their guiding light or residue
remains a beacon
a searchlight that still scans the heavens
in search of that bright beam
                              that went ahead.

FOR A FRIEND

Hale Matthews, full of grace
when Helen rang me with the news
I felt I'd never smile again.
For if anyone brought laughter
                          to my life
or taught me how to smile
                  at my own actions
and myself, it was you.

You only let me boast so much
before you knocked the stuffing
                          from my shirt.

Every time I laugh
or make rejoicing sounds
I'll remember
that all the best laughs
and the best times I knew,
            coming of age,
originated and were had with you.

Friend, rest peaceably.
Though I know you won't.
You'll tickle angels till they giggle
or outdistance devils in their race.

Hail, Hale Matthews!
Truly, you were full of grace.

THE POET

He knew that life hangs on
         for each of us
only as long as we are able
         to be understood.
For him it was enough
if now and then a truth
bubbled to the surface
and made a little headway
through that day's lies.

And so his words and work
stayed largely private
         and unrecognized
except by those of us
to whom with age
truth becomes a way
         of reconciliation.

His last book
was the hardest
to get out of him
        and onto paper
for he had finally reached that time
            all authors pray for
when the lack of any need to compromise
                    takes over.
And so it was the verses contained therein
            were longer in the making,
                    and his best.

Why is it
people send me poems,
he once crankily said to me.
Don't they know that in this little life
there is barely time to get my own words
            down on the page.

They believe in you,
I tried to reassure him.
Your opinion is their opiate.

Bullshit he replied
with unpoetic grandeur.
They seek a testimonial
and fill my postbox up with trash.

What about encouragement,
                    I argued.
He thought a moment
then without a smile opined,
ballroom dancers should be stopped
whenever they attempt *Swan Lake*.

JAMES WRIGHT, 1927–1980

He heard the earth
            grumbling and rejoicing
because his inner ear
was fine-tuned to a fraction.
Plain or fancy he always saw the sky
because he could not be induced
to wear a set of blinders
no matter who came forward
with the bit and harness.
Given the choice to set his sights
            far off on posterity
or near and now on people,
for him it was no choice,
people won the day
            and his attention.

And the ground became richer
and the sky grew wider
and those people he trapped in a pose
gained posterity by being trapped
                inside the poet's eye.
He promised us
the branch would never break
and even at his death
the strongest wind does not start
                the tree to swaying.
Why? Because not even God
would aid in breaking
an honest poet's promise.

MURIEL RUKEYSER, 1914–1980

She is there
somewhere still, I think
fighting for roses,
pruning the suckers
that battle new shoots
for what energy
        the taproot offers
the way she pruned
           unnecessary words
from sentences that strangle
        poems in their crib.

She is still there,
where language lurks
and night winds listen

She and I are joined
              in a way
end to end
with Charles Ives crowded in
                        between us.

Death did not carry her
anywhere but everywhere
She springs with spring
and causes all of us
to fight for roses.

PICTURE POSTCARD
for Margaret Blackstone

She stands beneath a tree
             that blossoms,
apple blossoms, I suppose.
A smile, an inner smile
             is somewhere there,
a laugh half opening, then gone.
Delicate. Shy. Stopped still
within a world
          that she made up.

But she only waits
          to lead you in,
and who would not come running
sneaking past the gate
and down into the orchard
she's made richer
by her dallying this day?

If I am passing by Meg's office
I never miss the chance
to pause within the doorway
just to reassure myself
the postcard is still there.
It always is.
A picture of the shy Edna Millay
                    reaching up
to touch an overhanging bough
of plum or apple blossoms.

No *drenched and dripping apple tree*
not in this tinted photograph;
only the bough that sunshine
burst from bud to blossom.

My appreciation
of the camera's blink
has never been so strong.
I have not marveled more
at the beauty of a tree
so filled with blossoms
it might lean and fall,
even when I stood
                in such an orchard
my own self.

Meg bends over piles of words
that crowd her desk
                like double anthills
and on the bookcase just in sight:
                        a picture postcard.

Now softly in the whisper
                    of a whisper
you can almost hear
the girl inside the postcard say,
I will be the gladdest thing
                    under the sun!
I will touch a hundred flowers
                    and not pick one.
And you believe her.

TO WHIT MAN

Only the smell of blood remains
where warriors last in the dooryard
                              bloomed
but though the enemy's been gone
                for twenty years or more
the smell is still as strong
as winds will let a smell be.

Strange how a battle haunts a house
and how participants long gone
still stay as ghosts within a garden.
That might explain why soldiers soldier—
perhaps they come from no place
loved enough to warrant a return,
hence the conquest and the haunting.

THE DAY AFTER THE FORTY-EIGHTH

Another table with wooden legs.
I walk from one room to another.
She walks away toward the city.
I am still alone. In a holding pattern.
One tenant in the now-built building
has greened his balcony with Astro-turf.
The moon is not up. And not coming.
Yesterday balloons arrived. In seven colors.
The elevator opened. It was empty.
I'm told she is not coming back.
The telephone. Dennis at this hour?
The Pepsi-Cola sign lights up.
The city lights up with it.
The building now obstructs the view.
I've started writing again.

The cats are scrambling to get out.
The heat's turned off. It must be Spring.
The landlord economizes. I think of moving.
They're tearing down the walls upstairs.
The cats are scratching to come in again
I must have missed the equinox
She's back. She speaks to me. I speak back.
We both say nothing. Words are vacant.
I am no longer obsessed or worry over
what goes on in the new building.
Maybe I will take an elevator ride.
Dennis calls and says
Write something nice about the rain.
My brother leaves for Costa Rica.
I write something nice about the rain.

I play again with crystal blocks.
Is that the moon? It is.
She asks if I will loan her money.
The noise upstairs is like a dozen drummers.
Someone jumped or fell from the roof
last night or early in the morning.
Icarus has blundered once again.
Dennis calls. I tell him *no*.
I am making a list of all my lists.
I wrote her a check in blood red ink.
Some birds I had not seen before appear.
The room is wider. The maid's been here.
I am not partial to the month of May.
Outside another balcony is greened.
Dennis calls. I answer, *maybe*.

The girl is back. She brought a rose.
God climbs the stairs for exercise.
An anthill menaces the master bedroom.
Astronauts buried my book on the moon.
The cats are chasing their own tails.
The telephone rings and rings and rings.
I am not writing. The words fail.
Nicki claws at the last balloon.
The girl keeps waving the birds away.
The L in the Pepsi-Cola sign is out.
My brother's plane has been delayed.
I'm told it's only another revolution.
Finally the last balloon explodes.
Dennis is standing outside in the hall.
A table with wooden legs. Nothing changes.

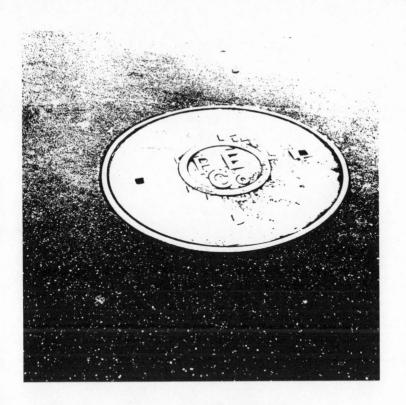

part the fifth:

nine songs

FOR BRUCE BOWDEN

*Unless otherwise noted
the music meant to accompany
these lyrics was composed by
the author.*

THE HUNTERS

The Hunters come, the Hunters go
down dark streets dancing
to the only tunes they know.
And like the does in morning
that feed along the lake
hearts are only underbrush
beneath their feet that break.
Don't worry the wind, didn't you know?
When the morning comes they'll go.

Run, lonesome lion,
don't be caught, frightened doe.
They aim their arrows straight
and they'll cut you down and go.

The Hunters smile, vacant smiles
and the promises they make
are only good a little while
For the hunter and the hunted
are really quite the same
and the hunting, not the loving
is the pleasure of the game.
Don't worry the wind, didn't you know?
When the morning comes they'll go.

Fly, bird, they're coming
and they'll catch you if they can
little fox, you're not so cunning
you can't fool the man.

I'M ALMOST THERE
(Music: Andre Popp)

I'm almost there, in fact, I can see it
I'm nearly where there is no turning back,
the darker it gets, the better I like it,
the better I like it, the darker it gets.

I'm almost there, in fact, I can see it
I'm nearly where there is no turning back,
the darker it gets, the better I like it,
the better I like it, the darker it gets.

Some men have questions they never ask
and so they never learn the answers,
some have suggestions so carefully masked
they spend their whole lives being dancers.

Where have you been throughout all my lifetime,
why did it take you so long to come near?
I'm almost there to start a new lifetime
I'm almost there, now that you're almost here.

Some men have speeches but they don't speak
and so they're never ever heard,
some men have passions so wan and weak
that no one ever gets the word.

I've heard the word and unmasked at the dancing,
I'm almost there and there's no turning back,
the darker it gets, the better I like it,
the better I like it, the lighter it gets.

I'm nearly there now that you're nearly here.

TO YOU
(Music: Jacques Brel)

I'd lie down in darkness with devils
and awaken with strangers
that I never knew,
I'd follow the hoofbeats of heartaches
if I thought they would lead me To You.

There's so little magic in morning
butterflies in your eyes and a teardrop or two,
I'd run down the dawning with danger
if I could be running To You.

If I cried out to God without warning
who am I, where am I
why am I so alone?
He'd probably show me the highway
leading To You and to home.

There's so little magic in midnight
fireflies in your eyes
and a sparkle or two,
I'd dance through the darkness with danger
If I could be dancing To You.

If love gives you life or takes lifetimes
I'll give life or take life to you.

"The sunlight, the moonlight
tries to make everything all right."

WE LIVE ON ISLANDS
(Music: Hildegard Knef–
Hans Hammerschmid)

We live on islands and that's at best,
so as sailors we know no rest.

To reach the mainland you run a lifetime
but one small lifetime is never enough.

The sirens, the saviors compete for our favors
always singing come to me (no)
come to me (no).

We live on islands, uncharted places,
forgotten countries forgotten faces.

The sunlight, the moonlight
tries to make everything all right
listen, come to me (please, no)
come to me (no, no).

Each man's an island keeping to himself
I'll show you my land if you'll show me your self.

I THINK OF YOU
(Music: Francis Lai)
for Petula Clark

When I'm alone at night
and there's no one to comfort me
I think of you
and suddenly my pillow
is your face and arms.

And when the winter wind
comes chasing after me
I think of you
and it's as though I've crawled beneath
a blanket soft and warm.

How did I get
from dark to daylight
till you happened to pass by?
How did I find my way through life
until you brightened up my sky?
Was there a sky at all
till you painted it for me?

How did I get on, till you came along?

Who knows how many times
I pause in every day
to think of you
as often as the sun sails out
upon the silent sea
and if you're wondering why it is
I only think of you
well it's because I'd like to be
as close to you,
as you've become to me
I think of you.
I think of you.

THE MARVELOUS CLOUDS

I'm the son of the wild swan of Flanders
who sailed on a river of dreams
my mother, the swan, has left me and gone
my home is the banks of the streams
and The Marvelous Clouds sail by
The Marvelous Clouds
aloft in the soft summer sky
The Marvelous Clouds.

I've seen all the lovers in doorways
I've heard every promise at dawn
I've spent too much time, just standin' in line
to be told I should move along
and The Marvelous Clouds sail by
The Marvelous Clouds
aloft in the soft summer sky
The Marvelous Clouds.

I've looked at the eyes of your heroes
as they sailed home from far distant lands
the mud on their uniforms, mud on their boots
blood on their faces and hands
and The Marvelous Clouds sail by
The Marvelous Clouds
aloft in the soft summer sky
The Marvelous Clouds.

My father the king of the mountain
looks down and watches his child
"Come home," says he, "if you hate what you see
you're young and the country is wild."
And The Marvelous Clouds
aloft in the soft summer sky
The Marvelous Clouds.

But I stay and I wait for the cannon
and the drums to stop drumming my ears
is it too late mankind, have you run out of time—
it's a matter of days and just years.
And The Marvelous Clouds sail by
The Marvelous Clouds
aloft in the soft summer sky
The Marvelous Clouds.

"*Cross the crossroads when you meet them . . .*"

MILES TO GO

Sleep in starlight, wake in sunshine
lullaby and don't you cry
tears are for the grown-up people
you've got miles to go untroubled
you've got miles to go.

Trace the clumsy cloud formations
celebrations in the sky
what was meant to come is coming
you've got miles to go untroubled
you've got miles to go.

There to pull you down
are people everywhere
you've got to plant your feet on the ground
and tell them, "I don't care."

Cross the crossroads when you meet them
and you'll meet them by and by
every mile's another milestone
you've got miles to go untroubled
you've got miles to go.

God's been busy building highways
you've got miles to go untroubled
you've got miles and miles to go.

SLEEP WARM

I sleep safely, I sleep soundly
knowing you sleep warm
even if you're rolling in
somebody else's arms.

I sleep easy, I sleep gently
knowing you sleep warm
even when I've lost you to
the darkness and the dawn.

That last full moon
was more than I could take
I willed myself asleep
I cried myself awake.

Still, I sleep easy, I sleep safely
knowing you sleep warm,
every night I still pretend
you're locked up in my arms.